S0-ABO-371

76524
Leach Library

DISCARD

LEACH LiBRARY
276 Mammoth Road
Londonderry, NH 03053
432-1127

DISCARD

Leach Library
276 Mammoth Road
Londonderry, NH 03053

Adult Services 432-1132
Children's Services 432-1127

Of Things
Natural,
Wild, and Free

Of Things Natural, Wild, and Free

A Story about Aldo Leopold

by Marybeth Lorbiecki

illustrated by Kerry Maguire

A Carolrhoda Creative Minds Book

Carolrhoda Books, Inc./Minneapolis

J
PIO
LEO

oo Junes
Lerner
2127(1595)

For Dad and Mom
—thanks for the camping, canoeing, and tramps
in the woods (among endless other things)—and
in honor of my grandfathers, for their examples
of gentle, loving strength

My gratitude to Curt Meine, who introduced me to Aldo, inspired me to write this book, and served as a resource along the way; to Nina Leopold Bradley, for sharing loving memories of her father and giving me access to family papers and photographs; and to Robert A. McCabe. Thanks also to Bernie Schermetzler of the University of Wisconsin Archives; Betty Beck and Helen Parsons of the Des Moines County Historical Society; Gary Laib, Paula Schanilec, Lisa Morris Kee, and Gaylord Nelson.

Note: Aldo's real name was Rand Aldo Leopold. While he was still an infant, his family dropped "Rand" from his name.

Text copyright © 1993 by Marybeth Lorbiecki
Illustrations © 1993 by Carolrhoda Books, Inc.,

All rights reserved. No part of this book may be reproduced, stored in a retrieval system, or transmitted in any form or by any means, electronic, mechanical, photocopying, recording, or otherwise, without the prior written permission of Carolrhoda Books, Inc., except for the inclusion of brief quotations in an acknowledged review.

Library of Congress Cataloging-in-Publication Data

Lorbiecki, Marybeth.
  Of things natural, wild, and free : a story about Aldo Leopold /
by Marybeth Lorbiecki ; illustrations by Kerry Maguire.
    p. cm. — (A Carolrhoda creative minds book)
  Includes bibliographical references (p.   ).
  Summary: A biography of the pioneer in wildlife conservation and author of "A Sand County Almanac."
  ISBN 0-87614-797-X
  1. Leopold, Aldo, 1887-1948—Juvenile literature. 2. Naturalists—Wisconsin—Biography—Juvenile literature. [1. Leopold, Aldo, 1887-1948. 2. Naturalists.] I. Maguire, Kerry, ill. II. Title. III. Series.
QH31.L618L67 1993   92-44049
    333.95'16'092—dc20   CIP
  [B]   AC

Manufactured in the United States of America

1 2 3 4 5 6 98 97 96 95 94 93

Table of Contents

Woodscraft and Honor   7

To Be a Forester   13

Leather Chaps and a
   Ten-Gallon Hat   20

Matters of Life and Death   25

There's More to a Forest
   than Trees   32

Starting a Science   39

Ecology in Practice   47

The Moral of It All   54

Afterword   61

Bibliography   63

① Woodscraft and Honor

Eight-year-old Aldo walked quietly along the path, trying not to rustle the leaves. Suddenly his father, Carl Leopold, stopped and flipped a rotting log. Spud barked excitedly. Underneath the log was a tuft of brown fur, a trail of slender pawprints, and a pile of crayfish skeletons. What had lived here? It had to be a mink.

Aldo's father could read stories from the land like other people could read them out of books. Carl had once been a traveling salesman. He had journeyed over the midwestern territories by buckboard and by foot, selling barbed wire and roller skates. He had hunted, camped, and lived off the land. Now at each Sunday picnic, Carl led his children on nature walks to teach them the ways of the woods, prairies, and swamps.

Aldo absorbed his father's words. He asked question after question and dreamed of living his father's adventures.

On Saturdays, while his father was out hunting, Aldo would cross the yard to the Big House. There his grandparents, Opa and Oma Starker, lived. Their mansion crowned Prospect Hill, overlooking the Mississippi River and Burlington, Iowa.

Opa had come from Germany as a young architect and landscape engineer. Over the years, he had become one of Burlington's most successful businessmen. Now retired, he tended his gardens and his grandchildren. Aldo would trail after Opa, learning how to grow trees, flowers, and vegetables. Opa spoke German and always carried his pruning shears in his pocket. Each year he recruited Aldo and his family to help with his spring planting, when he transformed his yard into a lush bluffside park.

Born January 11, 1887, Aldo was the oldest of the Leopold children. He led his sister, Marie, and his brothers, Carl and little Frederick, on grand escapades. They skated on the river, trapped rabbits, and collected plants. There were riotous snowball fights and free-for-all baseball games. At night the Leopolds would gather in the Starker parlor. The light from gas lamps flickered in huge mirrors as Aldo's mother played the piano and everyone sang. The smell of German pastries hung in the air. Aldo had a lively sweet tooth, and he'd snitch treats when no one was looking.

When Aldo started school, he could speak both English and German. He excelled in his classes but liked exploring better. He and his Irish spaniel, Spud, would take off to examine the riverbanks, the bluffs, and the sloughs. Sometimes Aldo got so caught up in his adventures, he skipped school.

A steady stream of traffic passed below Aldo's home on the bluff. Tugboats guided enormous log rafts, and steamboats carried well-dressed passengers. Overhead, flocks of migrating birds flew north or south, depending on the season. Birds were Aldo's specialty. At eleven, he listed in a notebook the thirty-nine bird species he had seen. "I like wrens," he wrote, "because they do more good than almost any other bird, they sing sweetly, they are very pretty, and very tame." Aldo hated crows and English house sparrows, though, because they pestered his songbirds. He'd take after them with rocks or a slingshot.

The best time of the year for Aldo came in August. That's when the Leopolds and Starkers traveled to an island resort on Lake Huron called Les Cheneaux. The island was ideal for exploring. It was nearly wild. Woods covered the land, and there were no roads. Walking trails connected the clubhouse, tennis courts, and golf course. Groceries were towed out by boat.

Aldo tramped over the island paths, making maps of the hills and plants. His eyes scanned the woods for birds and animal signs. Often he, his father, and Carl, Jr., would go fishing or camp out for three or four days. The "men" made it their challenge to live off the land. Blueberries and beach plums spiced up their morning pancakes. A touch of squirrel meat or trout added zest to their rice-and-potato stews.

The Les Cheneaux trip always ended too quickly. But once they were back in Iowa, it was hunting time. On Saturdays Aldo's father woke him long before sunup. Calling their dogs, the two walked down to the train station. It was a quick trip to one of the hunting clubs on the Illinois side of the river. By sunrise they were perched atop a muskrat mound or squatting in the mud, waiting for ducks.

Since there were few hunting laws in the late 1800s, hunters baited hungry birds with corn and shot them in huge flocks. Birds of all kinds, from eagles to pigeons, were killed by the wagonload. Aldo's father bristled over these unsportsmanlike actions. He set his own rules and limits. Carl never hunted in the spring, when the number of birds was the lowest. He didn't use baits. He always followed wounded animals to put them out of pain. He never shot for trophies, and he stopped hunting rare animals altogether. Wild game was a big treat in the Leopold and Starker households. Yet Carl never brought home more than the family could eat in a week.

Carl passed on his hunting rules to his children. For many years, Carl made Aldo carry a stick that had been carved to look and feel like a gun. Aldo had to prove he could tote the stick all day without getting careless. Then, around the age of eleven, he was awarded a single-shot shotgun. He learned to make each shot count. "Never point a gun at anything you don't intend to kill" was Carl's stern law.

As the seasons changed, so did Aldo's activities. Just after his thirteenth birthday, though, Aldo's life shifted painfully. Opa and Oma died, a few months apart. His family moved into the Big House, and Aldo entered high school.

Burlington High was overcrowded, and Aldo was too shy to stand out. He observed everyone with his serious blue-green eyes, but said little. He preferred to escape by streetcar to Flint Creek to watch kingfishers and crayfish. Although the school was known for its difficulty, Aldo rose to the top of his class (except in math). English, history, and biology suited him best. He devoured stories of sportsmen and adventurers, explorers and scientists. He collected favorite quotations and kept journals of his observations of nature.

Aldo's mother, Clara, doted on her eldest. She didn't want all the time he spent outside to roughen him, so she pressed him into reading novels, poetry, plays, and philosophy (which he liked). She even forced him into dance lessons (which he didn't like). But nothing could take the outdoors out of Aldo.

Since his father ran the Leopold Desk Company and it depended on wood, Aldo paid attention to the lumber industry. The nation's forests were being cut faster than they could grow back. The United States had begun to set aside forest reserves to protect the trees in the 1890s. Then, while Aldo was in high school, one of the country's first forestry schools opened at Yale University. Aldo knew immediately what he wanted to do. If he could become a forester, he could get paid to work in the woods all day. For Aldo, a job couldn't get any better.

② To Be a Forester

In 1903, Aldo said good-bye to Burlington High. He was heading out East to a high-class boarding school. He figured if he could do well there, he ought to have a chance at Yale. Before he went, though, he wanted one last shot at adventure.

The Leopolds skipped Les Cheneaux that summer and loaded up their canvas tents for Estes Park, Colorado. When August came to a close, Aldo and his father left the family to travel north through Yellowstone Park. They joined two other fathers and sons for a big-game hunting trip in Montana.

On the trail, there was excitement around every turn. Geysers spewed steam, and rivers rushed through colored stone canyons. A bear stampeded their horses and later raided their supply wagon, leaving behind a trail of half-eaten sausages. Afterward a blizzard locked them in camp. No one shot much. By trip's end, though, Aldo had added forty new bird species to his list.

When Aldo returned home, he had to get ready for school. Lawrenceville Preparatory School was several hundred miles away, amid New Jersey pasturelands, marshes, and wooded ridges. Aldo arrived there by train on January 6, 1904, five days before his seventeenth birthday. Within two days, he was tramping about the countryside.

The move wasn't easy. It was Aldo's first time away from his family, and he didn't fit in at Lawrenceville. He was a half year behind his class, and his midwestern accent sounded strange to his eastern and southern classmates.

Aldo, however, was unusual enough to be interesting. His classmates nicknamed him "the Naturalist" and teased him constantly. Aldo held himself proudly aloof. He saw himself as more studious than the rest. Soon, though, some of the fellows were asking to come with him on his hikes.

They thought it would be good for some laughs. But they got caught up in the explorations too. And Aldo found they weren't such bad fellows after all.

While Aldo was away at Lawrenceville, his mother waited daily for the mail. Aldo penned so many letters home that writing became a lifelong habit. He'd write pages and pages, detailing the discoveries he'd made and the birds he'd seen.

Few things escaped Aldo's notice during his woodland tramps. He knew the habits of some birds so well that he worried when they didn't arrive back from migration at their usual time. On April 13, 1904, he wrote home:

There I was, walking along and just thinking of the overdue birds, when far away up the stream I heard the rattle of a kingfisher. . . . I made a record going up the bank of that creek. And when I arrived, sure enough, he was there, rattling and plunging in true kingfisher fashion. It would be putting it tamely to say I felt relieved.

Migrating birds were on his father's mind too. Carl was back in Iowa, pushing for state laws to protect the birds. But other hunters were fighting against him. Aldo understood. He wrote to his father:

> I am very sorry that the ducks are being slaughtered as usual, but of course could expect nothing else. When my turn comes to have something to say and do against it..., I am sure nothing in my power will be lacking to the good cause.

For the time being, however, Aldo's hours were filled with tramping through the woods, playing baseball, running track, skipping class (when he could afford to), and a lot of studying. Aldo did so well in his courses that the fellows called him "the Shark." (But mathematics still got the best of him.) Aldo caught up to his classmates and graduated with them. He sailed through Yale's entrance exams and was on his way.

The forestry program at Yale was for graduate students only. So Aldo enrolled in college courses at the Sheffield Scientific School on the Yale campus to earn his undergraduate degree. He moved into a room at 400 Temple Street and started studying physics, chemistry, mechanical drawing, and geometry. All at once, he had little time for bird watching and plant collecting. He had tiptoed into the world of dances, football games, yachting, fraternities, and parties. He changed from a penny-pincher who liked his old field clothes to what his brother Frederick called "a dude." Aldo stood out on campus as the man with the striped tailored suits and the jazzy ties. "He didn't think he was cut from the common cloth," said Frederick, "and he wasn't."

Though Aldo had discovered a taste for fancy clothes and high-class doings, he hadn't completely stopped his outdoor explorations. Aldo befriended a boy named Bennie Jacobosky, whose parents had little money and little time for their son. Aldo showed Bennie the woods, and Bennie showed Aldo how people who were less fortunate often lived. Aldo began to see himself as someone who had "received everything and done little."

To make up for his good fortune, Aldo drove himself hard, trying to prove his worth. In his third year at Sheffield, his discipline cracked. He discovered that college women were far more interesting than college courses. Aldo cut classes and stopped studying. Eventually the college dean threatened to kick him out of school. His parents threatened to cut the purse strings.

Aldo got the message. He quit going to dances. He quit attending football games. His only time outdoors was put to chopping, thinning, surveying, and mapping trees. He passed his final exams and received a bachelor's degree in June 1908. The next fall, he officially entered the Yale Forestry School for a one-year master's degree program.

The end was finally in sight. He joined the Foresters' Society of Robin Hood and let Yale form him into the perfect ranger.

③

Leather Chaps
and a Ten-Gallon Hat

By the time Aldo graduated from the Yale
Forestry School in 1909, the United States Forest
Service managed over 150 million wooded acres.
Gifford Pinchot, the service's director, looked at
the forests like a bank account. They made money
for the country when trees were sold for timber
and permits were sold for grazing livestock. The
ranger's job was to manage these sales and protect
the forests from fire and disease. A healthy crop
of trees had to be saved in the national account.

The Forest Service hired young Leopold shortly
after his graduation. It sent him off to the wilds
of District 3—to the Apache National Forest in
Arizona Territory. This forest had only been protected as a national reserve for one year. Previ-
ously the area had belonged to the Apaches, and
the lands were still wild.

No roads crossed the Apache. One could only get there by stagecoach and horse. Leather chaps and a ten-gallon hat were necessities. Aldo spent his first paycheck on them, as well as on blue jeans, a pair of revolvers, a saddle, and a horse.

Aldo swaggered around the forest lands, climbing mountains and flicking fishing lines into rushing streams. He lived with the other bachelor foresters in an adobe bunkhouse. Together the men fought fires, made deals with loggers, played sandlot baseball, and lived the cowboy life.

When they had a chance, the rangers shot mountain lions, wolves, and grizzly bears. They figured the more predators they killed, the safer the cattle and sheep would be—and the more deer, elk, and bighorn sheep there would be. Many of these large game animals were becoming scarce, and Aldo and the other foresters wanted to protect their numbers. They arrested anyone they caught hunting game illegally. But there were too many acres to watch over and too few hunting laws.

A month after his arrival, Aldo got his first big assignment. He took over the leadership of a crew mapping timber on the Apache's Blue Mountain Range. This group of "timber cruisers" were old hands. Aldo stuck out as the "tenderfoot" from the first. He got lost more than once. He abandoned camp to chase after illegal hunters or to do some hunting himself. He miscalculated surveys and acted as if he knew everything.

Aldo's supervisor, Arthur Ringland, heard a round of complaints when the group returned. He called for an investigation. Cocky and conceited, Aldo welcomed it. He thought an investigation would clear his name. It only smirched it more. Fortunately for Aldo, the Forest Service decided his mistakes grew out of inexperience. They gave him one more chance.

The next summer, Aldo led a new team of timber cruisers. This time the crew members were more inexperienced than he was. And Aldo had learned from his mistakes. He measured more carefully, guided his group more efficiently, laughed more often, and carried a humbler opinion of himself.

In March of 1911, Arthur Ringland called Aldo to the district's headquarters in Albuquerque. Arthur wanted to get to know this young forester a little better before deciding his next post.

Aldo found it exciting to be back in a town again. He was loafing about a drugstore with

Ringland when Anita and Estella Bergere walked in—two dark-haired, dancing-eyed beauties. Ringland introduced Aldo to the women, and within the week, the two foresters were invited to a party at the Bergere home in Santa Fe. Both men gladly accepted.

The night they arrived, the ranch was all lit up with paper lanterns. Young women in colorful dresses wove in and out of the crowds with their own small bird-shaped lamps. Estella came over to Aldo and handed him her parrot. This was clearly an invitation to dance. Aldo smiled and took her hand.

The twenty-year-old schoolteacher had a gentle, laughing way about her. No one is sure what Aldo said to Arthur Ringland after that dance, but "Ring" got the message. He assigned Aldo to the Carson National Forest—the closest forest to Santa Fe and Estella Bergere.

4

Matters of
Life and Death

Aldo returned to the Apache to pack his gear and sell his horse. On the way to his new post, Aldo stopped in Santa Fe. Afterward he wrote to his sister, "Estella is a wonder on a horse, and...she is very much of a peach." Aldo had only one concern. Estella was seeing someone else. And Aldo was stationed a whole day's train ride away. The best he could do would be to woo her by mail.

Aldo railroaded on to the Carson. He was stricken with disappointment. This forest was far tamer than the Apache. Too many sheep and cattle had grazed the Carson's lands. Aldo wrote, "There is practically no game in this country. Of course the sheep have run out all the deer."

Aldo and his boss, Harry C. Hall, had been hired to stop the overgrazing. They were to grant fewer grazing permits and promptly arrest offenders. They slung pistols from their hips to show the

25

ranchers and herders they meant business.

Aldo's pen, though, became his most forceful tool. He started a newsletter for rangers called the *Carson Pine Cone.* Aldo used it to "scatter seeds of knowledge, encouragement, and enthusiasm." Most of the *Pine Cone*'s articles, poems, jokes, editorials, and drawings were Aldo's own. His readers soon realized that the forests' animals were as important to him as the trees. His goal was to bring back the "flavor of the wilds."

In the fall, Ring paid Aldo an unexpected visit to bring him news—Estella's beau had proposed. Now love letters weren't enough. Aldo made a mad dash to offer his own passionate marriage proposal.

Estella was overcome. She needed time to think. For almost three months, letters passed back and forth. Aldo had trouble concentrating. Finally, he returned to Santa Fe for an answer.

Estella said yes. Aldo was so happy, he could think of nothing to say when he wrote home.

A few months after his engagement, twenty-five-year-old Aldo was promoted to acting supervisor. He was busier than ever, working with the cowmen and sheepers. In his free time, he built a new home looking out over the Rio Grande Valley. Aldo brought his new bride back to this little house in October 1912. Estella learned to hunt, skin, and cook with Aldo at her side. In the evenings, the newlyweds read to each other by the firelight.

The Leopolds discovered in the spring that they were expecting a child. Estella decided to visit her family while Aldo attended to sheep business in a distant section of the forest. He rode from one lambing area to the next, camping under the stars. Unfortunately, the stars were not out most of those April evenings. A storm hit. It sleeted, snowed, hailed, and rained for two days. Aldo slept curled up in a soaked bedroll. Then, shivering, he climbed on his horse and rode toward the nearest railway tracks to flag down a train.

As he rode, Aldo's legs swelled so much he had to slash his boots open. An Apache found him wandering aimlessly. The man gave him food and a warm place to sleep. Eventually Aldo straggled into Chama, New Mexico, where a doctor gave him medicine for swollen joints. Aldo thought he would recover.

But he didn't. By the time he arrived back at Carson headquarters, he was so swollen he could hardly move. His assistant, Ray Marsh, insisted he see a doctor in Santa Fe. If Aldo had not taken his advice, he would probably have been dead within the week. His kidneys had failed. Deadly poisons were building up in his blood and muscles.

The doctor sent him to bed immediately. Estella and the Bergeres piled blankets on top of him and gave him "sweating pills." Slowly, Aldo's body rid itself of the poisons, and his kidneys began cleaning his blood once again.

His healing, though, only inched forward. Aldo remained in bed for six weeks. He lost weight, and his body failed to gain strength. Ray Marsh took over Aldo's duties at the Carson.

On June 6, 1913, Estella and Aldo took a train to Burlington. Aldo could do little more at his old home than sit on the Leopold porch with his pipe and a book. He watched the birds and thought about his life. He still had not done what he had set out to do—protect wild birds and game animals. Up to now, he had had big plans, but no time. Now all he had was time.

So he wrote articles for the *Pine Cone*, urging his fellow foresters to work for the health of the whole forest. He proposed that the forest animals could and should be managed just like the trees. In the fall, big news showed up in the *Pine Cone*. On October 22, 1913, Estella gave birth to a boy.

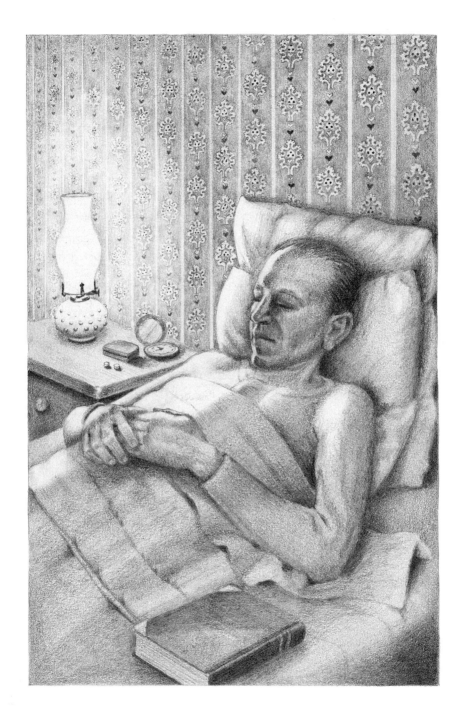

His name was Aldo Starker Leopold. No one could have been prouder than the baby's father.

Aldo and Estella traveled back to New Mexico to show off their son to the Bergeres. A full year after his illness, Aldo was still weak. His final leave of absence from the Forest Service ran out in May 1914. Aldo was out of a job. Now he and his family had to live off the generosity of the Leopolds and Bergeres. Aldo felt helpless.

In June, his doctor called him back to Burlington. Carl, Sr., had just had surgery, and the two of them could recover together. Aldo's spirits, though, were low and dipping lower.

Arthur Ringland wanted Aldo back in the Forest Service as badly as Aldo wanted to return. A letter arrived from Arthur describing a desk job in the district's grazing office. Aldo snatched the opportunity. It wasn't the job he wanted, but it was a job.

Aldo, Estella, and one-year-old Starker moved into a small house in Albuquerque. Aldo gardened, built wooden toys and decoys, studied Spanish with Estella, and played with Starker. He tried to forget the endless paperwork at his job.

One night in December, a telegram arrived. Carl Leopold, Sr., had died.

Aldo knew he could wait no longer to act. He had promised his father he would do something for the wild creatures they both loved. The time had come.

⑤

There's More to a Forest than Trees

Less than a month after his father's death and a few days before his twenty-eighth birthday, Aldo handed in a memo to his supervisors. It outlined ways to increase the number of game animals in the forests. His note was read and passed on to Washington, D.C. Not a single policy changed.

More than ever, Aldo wanted out of his job. But where was he to go? Arthur Ringland came to the rescue again. He designed a job just for Aldo. Aldo would develop programs and guidelines for game protection, publicity, and public recreation for the forests of District 3.

On June 15, 1915, Aldo peered down at the Grand Canyon. Billboards and electric lights dotted the rim. Shopkeepers with megaphones yelled at tourists on horses and in Model Ts. Garbage piled up everywhere, and sewage drained into the river. The destruction was appalling.

Aldo wanted tourists to be able to enjoy the

canyon without spoiling it. Over the next two years, he worked with the local forest supervisor on a plan to develop more effective campgrounds, trails, and rules for recreation.

After his visit to the canyon, Aldo plotted out areas in District 3 that could be laid out as bird sanctuaries or animal refuges. He wrote a wildlife management handbook for rangers. It described species, laid out new hunting and fishing laws, and explained methods of stocking animals and fish. This handy manual, the *Game and Fish Handbook*, was the first Forest Service book of its kind.

In October 1915, shortly after the manual was published, Aldo's second son, Luna Bergere Leopold, was born. Around the same time, the next step in Aldo's program began. He wrote letters to local sportsmen asking them to work together for the protection of game animals. Within months, Aldo was trekking through New Mexico and Arizona, organizing game-protection societies.

With quiet charm, enthusiasm, and logic, Aldo convinced sportsmen that they would soon have nothing to hunt if they did not work to save the wild animals that remained. Small conservation groups sprang up, and in March 1916, the New Mexico Game Protection Association was formed.

The members dedicated themselves to killing off the predators that stalked game animals, to enforcing stricter hunting laws, and to setting aside areas where game animals would be totally protected. Aldo became the group's secretary. Resurrecting an old title, Aldo produced a newsletter for interested foresters and hunters. The goal of the new *Pine Cone* was "to promote the protection and enjoyment of wild things."

In January 1917, near his thirtieth birthday, Aldo received a letter of congratulations from former president Theodore Roosevelt: "My dear Mr. Leopold, ... I think your platform simply capital.... Your association in New Mexico is setting an example to the whole country."

While game protection societies were springing up across the Southwest, war had exploded across Europe. The United States entered the fight in April 1917 to support the European allies against Germany. Conservation efforts were thrust aside. Forests were sliced up to make biplanes. Cattle slated for army rations overgrazed the forests' slopes and plains. Foresters became soldiers.

Aldo was not drafted because of his ill health. When the Chamber of Commerce in Albuquerque offered him a job as a spokesman, he took it.

For the next year and a half, Aldo spoke to all sorts of citizens and business groups, describing the delights of Albuquerque. He pressed the chamber to create more parks, to build in the style of traditional Hispanic architecture, and to hire a city planner.

In August 1917, Aldo toted Starker along on his first hunting trip and Aldo's first since his illness. That month he also celebrated the birth of his first daughter—Adelina, nicknamed Nina.

The war ended in November 1918, and the Forest Service rehired Aldo the next year. They placed him second in command of District 3, in charge of daily operations. It was his duty to inspect each of the district's forests to see they were running properly. At first, Aldo's supervisor didn't trust him to be thorough. So he had a hard-core army officer oversee Aldo and help him develop an eye for detail. Aldo was soon taking systematic notes on everything from logbooks to outhouses.

Aldo examined the southwestern forests so closely that he noted hillsides and riverbanks scarred by ravines. The cattle and sheep had eaten and ground the grasses down to nothing. The loose soil had been swept away by wind and driven by rain into rivers, muddying them up.

The mud was killing the fish, and the sun was baking the leftover soil into brick. Fewer and fewer plants could survive. The land was shifting into desert.

How could anyone stop the soil from being worn away? Erosion control soared to the top of Aldo's action list. He researched the topic and wrote the *Watershed Handbook*. This manual told foresters how to protect rivers and lakes by preventing soil erosion.

Each passing year as a forester had made Aldo see the forest as something more than just trees. There were the animals, grasses, rivers, lakes, and soil. Aldo envisioned still another quality of forests that needed protection—wildness itself. Throughout the country, places that were rare and spectacular were being ruined by human "improvements." Aldo began to wonder if the best use of these wild areas was no modern use at all. No roads. No grazing. No logging. No mining. No tourist cabins.

This was a shocking idea. Most people wanted to put every piece of land to some "use." Leopold teamed up with another forester, Arthur Carhart, to push for the protection of two specific wild places: the Gila Canyon area in New Mexico and

Trappers Lake in Colorado. Aldo set out to change a nation's mind about what its remaining patches of wilderness were for. He delivered speeches and wrote articles about the "wilderness idea." Wild places could not be grown like timber, he argued. They could only be saved from destruction.

At thirty-seven, Aldo was respected nationally, and even internationally, in forestry and conservation. The Forest Service wanted Aldo to put his skills to use as the assistant director of the Forest Products Laboratory in Madison, Wisconsin. The service hinted that if Aldo took the job, he would soon be promoted to director.

Perhaps Aldo felt he had accomplished all he could in a field position. Or maybe Aldo was looking for the scientific challenges a laboratory would offer him. He might even have been pressured into taking the job. But Aldo's days as a field forester ended. He accepted the job.

On June 3, 1924, five days after Aldo left the Southwest, one of his biggest triumphs occurred— the Forest Service approved of his plan for the Gila Wilderness Area. This was the first wild place to be so protected by the United States Forest Service. For this reason, Aldo earned the title "father of the national wilderness system."

6

Starting a Science

The sun glinted off Lake Wingra. Boys with fishing poles and stringers of sunfish dotted the shore. The children will like Madison, Aldo thought. But Estella won't. No more warm winters, adobe homes, red-tiled roofs, chickens in the yard, or Spanish on the tongue. Instead, it would be months of freezing, red brick and cement with neat, green lawns, and everything in English.

But even Estella cheered up when the family, which now included four-year-old Aldo Carl, bought a stucco home on Van Hise Avenue. Aldo led the family in a spring planting of trees, bushes, and wildflowers. They hung birdhouses and feeders, and explored the city's lakes.

At the laboratory, the odors of wood glues and varnishes bit the stale air. It was hardly the place for Aldo. He preferred a live tree in the forest to a tin of shavings in an experiment.

For the next four years, though, he directed

research and helped discover new uses for the otherwise wasted parts of trees and lumber. This work didn't make him happy. The best part of his day began in the evening at Van Hise Avenue. He and Estella would listen to classical music, and Aldo would quiz the kids about the interesting things they had done and learned during the day. On winter evenings, he'd go down to his basement workshop. There, he carved, sanded, glued, and balanced his own bows and arrows for hunting. He taught the rest of the family to make their own archery gear too.

On Sundays, the Leopolds often packed up their gear for a picnic in Wingra Park. They roved the grounds, choosing targets for their arrows. (Estella became so skilled that she won archery tournaments and taught classes in archery at the university.) There were family campouts and hunting trips. About once a year, Aldo and his brothers got together for a week-long canoe trip. And in 1929, a final member joined the family—little Estella. She too grew up surrounded by the smells of oak smoke from campfires and damp leaves in the woods.

Aldo, of course, had never stopped working to protect game animals and preserve the wilderness.

He was a leader in the American Game Association as well as other national scientific organizations. He had also joined several conservation groups in Wisconsin. Aldo, however, could live off of his hobbies for only so long. He needed work that meant something to him.

The Sporting Arms and Ammunition Manufacturers' Institute approached him with an unusual job offer. This group of gun and bullet makers wanted to make sure the sport of hunting didn't die out. So they asked Aldo to examine the conservation methods being used in the United States to see which worked best for game animals. It was a risky proposal. No one had ever tried such a project before, and if the institute didn't like Aldo's findings or methods, it would be free to fire him after a year.

Despite the risk, forty-one-year-old Aldo accepted the job. He started in July 1928 by visiting Minnesota and Michigan. For a few weeks or more, he traveled through each state in his beat-up Ford. He talked to lawmakers, foresters, farmers, businesspeople, and hunters. As he examined the midwestern states, he saw a trend. Wherever there was "clean" farming, few wild birds and other animals thrived. But wherever farmers had left grasses near fences, woods, and swamps for cover and food, wildlife was plentiful.

Aldo returned to Madison between trips. The University of Wisconsin had lent him a small office, and he had hired a part-time secretary. Every time he came back, he gave her mounds of notes, letters, and reports to be typed. He was also at work polishing the first chapters of a book project—"Deer Management in the Southwest."

As the 1920s came to an end, a time of hardship hit, later known as the Great Depression. Banks and businesses across the country closed. Many farmers lost their land. Thousands of people were out of jobs and broke. Conservation efforts were again shoved aside.

Aldo's *Report on a Game Survey of the North Central States* was published in 1931. It was the most in-depth summary of the state of American wildlife that had ever been published. Instantly Aldo became *the* expert in the new field of game conservation and management.

The *Survey* had answered questions about the Midwest, but funds to survey other areas ran low. Aldo knew he would need a new job soon. He decided to scrap the "Deer Management" project and assemble the scientific information he had gathered into a textbook, *Game Management.*

To test some of his management methods, Aldo formed the Riley Game Cooperative. He convinced a group of hunters and farmers to improve the farmers' lands for wildlife. The farmers agreed to leave brush piles, grasses, and trees on the edges of their fields, and to plant plots of crops for grouse, quail, and pheasants. The hunters chipped in money and hard work.

The experiment succeeded. No longer did the farmers have trouble with trespassing hunters. The hunters had a great place to hunt, and the farmers made extra money. Even better, more wild birds lived in the area than had lived there in years.

In July, Aldo attended a scientific conference on plant and animal population cycles. He met some of the world's greatest minds in biology and "ecology." This new science studied the connections between living things and their natural surroundings. Aldo's horizons broadened immeasurably. Now he was pondering how the cycles of plants, animals, fish, insects, diseases, and weather affect each other. His focus shifted from saving game animals and songbirds to saving all animals— and all the interconnected "cogs and wheels" in nature's system.

Less than a year later, the funding for Aldo's game-management work was cut. He was on his own. A publishing company agreed to publish *Game Management* if Aldo could finish it quickly and help pay the costs. It was another big risk. But Aldo pulled five hundred dollars from his savings and went to work full time on the book.

Estella probably felt the money worries the most since she had to make ends meet. For the next year and a half, the family scraped by on savings, money from Leopold stocks, and possibly small gifts from their relatives in Iowa and New Mexico.

Aldo received job offers. He refused them. He didn't want to move the family or quit working on the book. He was too close to finishing. The book was dedicated to his father, "a pioneer in sportsmanship." He completed it in July 1932.

Aldo had been aiming for a position at the University of Wisconsin. He wanted to do field research and train game-management professionals. But the university lacked funds. So Aldo became a consulting forester. He advised landowners and states on how to manage their land for the best use of humans *and* wildlife. The United States was one of his clients. They asked him to direct soil-conservation efforts in the Southwest.

⑦

Ecology in Practice

By summer, *Game Management* was selling well. It had been praised by scientists and conservationists. In August the University of Wisconsin announced that it was starting a graduate program in game management. And they had hired the most qualified person in the country to direct it— Aldo Leopold. He became the nation's first professor in the new field.

The university expected Aldo to do more than just teach game management, however. It wanted him to teach all the citizens of Wisconsin how to put conservation into practice.

Aldo gave short radio talks on how to make backyards and farms appealing to wildlife. He set up research areas and recruited Youth Conservation Clubs to work with him. "We weren't simply field hands," wrote one member. We were supposed to do "deep digging" for facts—"to observe, to ask questions, and to try putting things together."

In January 1934, Aldo taught his first class to a group of young farmers. Shortly after he began teaching, Aldo was called briefly to Washington, D.C., by President Franklin D. Roosevelt. Roosevelt had selected Leopold to work with two other conservationists on the President's Committee on Wild Life Restoration. The three men argued briskly over the best methods to use. However, they managed to agree that the government should buy up land for bird sanctuaries and wildlife refuges. They also decided that more scientific research was needed.

In the spring, Aldo took on his first graduate student. In addition, he began planning a university arboretum with other faculty members. Arboretums are usually formal gardens with exotic trees and plants. Aldo and the committee had something different in mind. They wanted a land laboratory where students could study ecology and visitors could learn about Wisconsin's original plants and animals. Aldo stated: "The time has come for science to busy itself with the earth itself. The first step is to reconstruct a sample of what we had to start with."

On June 17, 1934, five hundred acres of ruined farmland were dedicated for the University of

Wisconsin Arboretum and Wild Life Refuge. Shortly afterward, the work began. Native trees, wildflowers, and grasses were collected and planted. Grape tangles and brush piles were built up. Wild birds and animals were released on the grounds.

That summer, rain did not come. Dust storms blasted across the plains. The winds moved like carpet sweepers, pulling up soil from fields and tossing it through windows, under doors, into animals' lungs. No one had ever seen anything like it. It was a national disaster. And it had been brought on by poor farming and grazing practices.

Aldo's radio talks boomed in popularity. He was invited to speak on a nationwide radio program. His classes filled up. Over 315 farmers signed up to work on a soil-conservation project he directed in Coon Valley, Wisconsin.

Nor had the debate over wilderness protection been overlooked. That fall, a forester named Bob Marshall wrote to Aldo about forming a national conservation group. These "spirited individuals" would fight for the freedom of the United States' last stretches of wilderness. Marshall asked Leopold to be a leader in this "Wilderness Society." Aldo replied that he was "more than glad to serve."

In January 1935, the day after his forty-eighth

birthday, Aldo found something he had been look-ing for long and hard—a plot of land he could afford to buy. He came home excited and exuber-ant. He piled his family into the station wagon to go see his treasure. All they found were eighty acres of sand, old corn rows, and broken-down fences. In the middle, not far from the river, sat an old chicken coop. The family nicknamed it "the Shack."

Over the winter months, they mucked out the Shack and laid down a clay floor. The boys raised a new roof and built a handsome fireplace. They planted sorghum as food for quail and pheasants.

Once summer showed its face, Aldo got so busy that the Shack was forgotten. He had been invited to go on a three-month trip to Germany to examine forestry and game-management methods.

The tours showed him that Germany's national forests contained little more than the spruce trees planted after logging. They grew straight and in rows. Deer came to feed at troughs. Pheasants wandered like farm geese. No wolves howled. The forests were as tame as house pets.

Aldo saw the Germans had managed nature so strictly it could no longer work on its own.

If game management was to be effective, Aldo realized, it had to respect nature and its wildness. The goal could not be *control* but to *work with* "things natural, wild and free." Aldo wrote, "Conservation is a state of harmony between man and the land. . . . Harmony with land is like harmony with a friend."

In the spring of 1936, Aldo and his family set to the real work of learning to live in harmony with a piece of land. With sharpened shovels, they planted a thousand white pine and a thousand red pine trees. They sunk juneberry, blackberry, nannyberry, and cranberry bushes into the sandy soil, along with mountain ash, Norway pine, and plum trees.

Everyone worked till they had blisters and backaches. When the hot, dry winds came, the plants dried out. The family hauled buckets of water from the river on weekends. Like the rest of the nation's farmers, though, the Leopolds watched their plants die. The dust storms kept on coming.

Despite it all, the family noticed a strange liking for the old Shack creeping up on them. There was always canoeing, swimming, fishing, watching birds, hunting, doing scientific studies, and watching over their plants. At night, the guitars came out. The kids would serenade Daddy as he wrote short notes in the Shack Journal.

Throughout that and all summers, Aldo kept up a steady pace at work. Still, he was always firm about weekend trips to the Shack: "Never take anything up there that is not *absolutely* necessary." No radios, gadgets, or fineries. Instead there was a hand pump for water, a Dutch oven for outdoor cooking, fishing rods, an ax, and shovels. The shelves, benches, and outhouse were built out of junk that floated down the river or was rescued from the local dump.

As the winter of 1936 approached, Aldo took a bow-hunting trip into the Sierra Madre Mountains of Mexico. This was a land that was still wild, free, and healthy. It had wolves, jaguars, deer, wild turkeys, thick-billed parrots, and trout. Aldo had never seen so much wildlife living together in such numbers. He suddenly understood that all he had ever seen was sick land.

This trip sealed the argument for Aldo. The United States *must* save its last bits of wilderness for science, if for nothing else. Without wild land for comparison, Aldo reasoned, scientists would never be able to diagnose when land was sick. Nor would they ever know what to do to cure it.

8

The Moral of It All

Click, click, click. Everyone knew by the snap of the metal heels against the floor that "the Professor" was coming. He strode into the room, a medium-sized man with a deep voice, a large nose and large ears, and serious, gentle eyes. Aldo's hair was thinning, and he wore spectacles, but he still liked a well-cut suit and a classy tie.

In his course Game Management 118, Aldo led his students out into the fields and woods. There he taught them to read animal and landscape signs, and to ask questions, as his father had taught him. One former student said that Professor Leopold "never tired of asking the questions that ended up blowing my mind."

Aldo had four graduate students in spring 1937 and about seventy students in his other courses. Things had gotten cramped in the Soils Building. The only space where they could dissect specimens was in the toolshed on top of a seed drill.

Aldo was content to "make shift with the way things are." But his students were not. One fall night they posted a guard at the basement door. Then they quietly packed up Aldo's office—furniture, files, books, paintings, and all.

The next day, when Aldo showed up for work, everything was missing. His students escorted him to 424 Farm Place. It was an old three-story frame house owned by the university. It had a porch, a greenhouse, wooden floors, and a fireplace. As he walked inside, Aldo saw, neatly arranged and waiting for him, all his things.

Aldo was shocked, to say the least—yet pleased. The place soon became quite homey for both the professor and his students. Aldo would rise early in the morning and go there to do his writing. By the time his secretary arrived at eight o'clock, he would have piles of yellow-pad pages to be typed.

In 1938, Aldo was put in charge of a full teaching department at the University, which he titled the Department of Wildlife Management. He renamed his introductory course Wildlife Ecology 118. His job, as he saw it, was "to teach the student to see the land, to understand what he sees, and to enjoy what he understands." He used the word "land" rather than "wildlife."

He felt that it included "all of the things on, over, or in the earth." "Wildlife," he wrote, "cannot be understood without understanding the land."

As the 1930s came to a close, Germany, which had tried to control its forests and wildlife, was trying to control the world. One of Germany's allies—Japan—invaded Hawaii on December 7, 1941. The United States entered World War II.

Luna and Carl enlisted. Luna got stationed in the States, and Carl in the war zone. Aldo's courses were almost empty. For the first time in ages, Aldo had a little time on his hands. He had been collecting his essays, articles, speeches, journal entries, and scientific field notes over the years. Now he started rewriting them into parts for a single book on the relationship between people and land. The question was: How could people live on land without spoiling it?

While working on the book, Aldo was also on the Wisconsin Conservation Commission. The commission faced an ongoing catastrophe. The state's timber wolves had been killed or run off. Because of this, the number of deer had ballooned. The deer were eating up the state's newly planted forests. Where food was scarce, deer were collapsing from starvation and disease.

Part of Aldo's solution was to bring back the wolves. He deeply regretted that he had once worked to kill them off. "I was young then and full of trigger-itch," he wrote. "I thought that because fewer wolves meant more deer, that no wolves would mean hunters' paradise." He hadn't known then how important every species was for a healthy land system and how each species had an undeniable right to exist.

Most people in Wisconsin refused to have wolves in the state. So the commission voted for a season during which hunters could shoot not only bucks but also does. The result—a slaughter in some areas and few kills in others. Deer lovers lashed out at Aldo, calling him "Bambi Killer."

Aldo had had trouble with his eyes and his health, but now things got worse. Aldo couldn't sleep. He worried about his sons, his students, the deer, the forests, the wolves, the wilderness, and the world in general. When the atomic bomb was dropped on Japan, Aldo was pained. He saw it as a distressing turning point in human history, where people could no longer control their own weapons.

Finally, peace treaties were signed. Carl made it home safely, and his father wept for joy. As the soldiers returned, Aldo was swamped with students.

A painful tic developed on one side of his face. When it hit, it was as if he had been "smashed over the head with a sledge hammer."

Aldo tried different methods to heal the problem: rest, less work, and finally surgery. But the pain increased. The doctor sent him to bed for a month. Then in September 1947, sixty-year-old Aldo traveled to the Mayo Clinic in Rochester, Minnesota, for major surgery. The tic went away, but so did all feeling on his face's left side. He drooled a little and had trouble concentrating.

His strength grew over the winter, but his eyes dried easily. He had to apply drops every few minutes. Then came more surgery. All the while, Aldo tried to fulfill his many responsibilities and get his book of essays published.

Aldo's place of rest and freedom was the Shack. After eleven years, the Leopold land had started to plant itself. Trees spread out above their heads. A prairie bloomed outside their door. Woodcocks danced in the grasses. Only a small patch of sand remained as it had been. Aldo had left it unplanted to tell the land's history.

At the end of February 1948, the United States government asked Aldo to be a representative at a United Nations conference on conservation. Aldo had reached the summit of his profession.

Two months later, Aldo received news that Oxford University Press was going to publish his book of essays. He dedicated it to "my Estella."

"There are some who can live without wild things," it began, "and some who cannot. These essays are the delights and dilemmas of one who cannot." The essays described what Aldo had noticed in nature over his lifetime. He explained what these observations had taught him about wildlife, wilderness, ecology, and life. He wrote, "When we see land as a community to which we belong, we may begin to use it with love and respect."

The weekend after Aldo heard from Oxford University Press, he and Estella packed up the car and drove to the Shack to celebrate and relax. Young Stella arrived from college to help sharpen the shovels and plant the trees.

It was Aldo's last spring planting. On Wednesday, April 21, 1948, Aldo Leopold died while fighting a neighbor's grass fire. He had suffered a heart attack. The *Wisconsin State Journal* wrote, "It is a tragedy...to lose him, his mind, and the good works for which the grandchildren of today's children might thank him."

Afterword

A Sand County Almanac, Aldo's book of essays, was published in 1949. Since then, over a million copies have been sold. The book has been hauled up mountains, trundled into canoes, and stored at bedside tables. It has been translated into Chinese, French, Russian, as well as other languages. It is one of the best-loved books ever written about the environment.

Aldo left behind more than his books. His children followed in his footsteps and have contributed greatly to the protection of "things natural, wild, and free." His students and readers have also carried on his work.

On June 17, 1984, the University of Wisconsin Arboretum and Wildlife Refuge celebrated fifty years of growth. One could look out and see the kind of forests, wild-grass prairies, and marshes that had once covered Wisconsin.

At the Shack, the trees grow so tall and thick that they have had to be thinned. Rare prairie wildflowers bloom near Aldo's favorite bench. Deer wander past. The old chicken coop has been named a National Historic Building, and the land is protected as part of the Leopold Memorial Reserve. It remains a land laboratory for wildlife managers and students of wildlife ecology.

The fight led by Aldo to save the U.S. wilderness goes on. Logging, mining, oil drilling, ranching, and building companies demand that no land should be left without "wise use." They do not see that land can have its own "uses" we can enjoy. At the same time, tourists fight to bring snowmobiles, power boats, three wheelers, and other motors into wilderness areas. They don't see the damage motors cause to the soil, water, plants, and wildlife. As Aldo would say, "It's enough to make you bite off ten-penny nails."

Aldo's final hope was that people would learn *how* to love the land. He believed that if we love the land, we will do what is right with it. His rule of thumb went something like this: an action is right when it tends to preserve the stability, health, and beauty of a land's natural systems. It is wrong when it tends to destroy them. He once wrote, "We shall never achieve harmony with the land, any more, than we shall achieve justice or liberty for people." But he added, "In these higher aspirations, the important thing is not to achieve, but to strive..."

Bibliography of Major Sources

Primary Sources

Bradley, Nina Leopold (daughter); interview with author, July 1991.

——; "Personal Reflections of a Daughter," unpublished speech given at 1991 meeting of the Soil and Water Conservation Society.

Leopold, Aldo; *A Sand County Almanac with Essays on Conservation from Round River.* New York: Ballantine Books, 1990.

——; *The River of the Mother of God and Other Essays.* ed. Susan L. Flader and J. Baird Callicott, Madison: University of Wisconsin Press, 1991.

Leopold, Frederick; "Recollections of an Old Member [of Crystal Lake Hunt Club]" speech given at club March 1977, Des Moines County Historical Society.

Leopold Papers; Madison: University of Wisconsin Archives.

McCabe, Richard E., ed. *Aldo Leopold: Mentor.* by his Graduate Students, Madison: Department of Wildlife Ecology, University of Wisconsin, 1988.

McCabe, Robert A. *Aldo Leopold: The Professor.* (reminiscences of an assistant and student) Amherst, Wisconsin: Palmer Publications, 1987.

Schoenfeld, Clay. "Aldo Leopold Remembered," *Audubon,* March-April, 1978.

Voegeli, Jim. "Remembering Aldo Leopold," a radio documentary with interviews of friends, family, and students.

Secondary Sources

Brower, Stephen R. "The Starker-Leopold Family" Research Paper, April 1980, Des Moines County Historical Society.

Flader, Susan L. "Aldo Leopold: A Historical and Philosophical Perspective," speech to the Des Moines County Historical Society, April 17, 1980.

Gibbons, Boyd. "A Durable Scale of Values," *National Geographic,* November 1981.

Kaufman, Sharon. "Built on Honor to Endure," speech given to Des Moines County Historical Society, September 16, 1986.

Meine, Curt. *Aldo Leopold: His Life and Work.* Madison: University of Wisconsin Press, 1988.

Tanner, Thomas, ed. *Aldo Leopold: The Man and the Legacy,* foreword by Stewart Udall. Ankeny, Iowa: Soil Conservation Society of America, 1987.

All quotations have been taken from one of the sources listed above.